POCKETBOOKS

by BroadStreet

# 2-minute Prayers for Boys

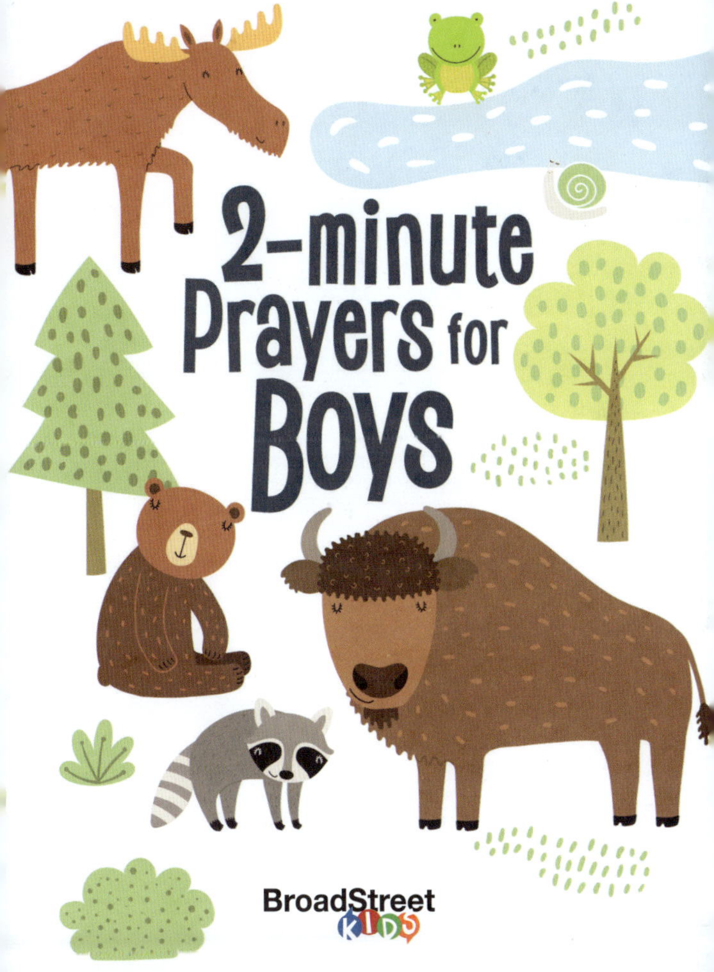

BroadStreet KIDS

BroadStreet Kids
Savage, Minnesota, USA
BroadStreet Kids is an imprint of BroadStreet Publishing Group, LLC.
Broadstreetpublishing.com

# 2-minute Prayers for Boys



9781424570959
9781424570966 eBook

Prayers composed by Jeanna Harder.



Typesetting and design by Garborg Design Works | garborgdesign.com
Editorial services by Michelle Winger | literallyprecise.com

Printed in China.

25 26 27 28 29 30 31 7 6 5 4 3 2 1

Dear God...

# Introduction

*"Heaven and earth will pass away. But my words will never pass away."*

MATTHEW 24:35 NIRV

Build a strong connection with God!

This pocketbook is packed with short, meaningful prayers and carefully chosen Scriptures to guide boys like you as you grow in confidence, courage, and faith.

Whether it's first thing in the morning, after school, or right before bed, this pocket prayer book helps you start talking with God.

Perfect for boys with busy days, big imaginations, and active lives, each prayer can be read in just a couple minutes.

Trust in God's love and find strength, wisdom, and bravery along the way.

DAY 1

# Happy People

*Happy are those who don't listen to the wicked,*
*who don't go where sinners go,*
*who don't do what evil people do.*

PSALM 1:1 NCV

God, I don't want to do bad things or lie and say mean words. That does not make you happy, and it doesn't make me happy either. I feel sad in my heart. Help me to pick good friends who I can trust. I want to make you proud of my good behavior and wise choices. I like being a happy person.

DAY 2

# He Saves Me

*God has saved us from deadly dangers. And he will continue to do it. We have put our hope in him. He will continue to save us.*

2 CORINTHIANS 1:10 NIRV

God, you have saved me from dangers that I don't even know about. This verse says that you will keep saving me. Thank you! You are my hero. When I start to feel worried or afraid, I will remember that you are bigger than my problems. You can handle any scary situation. Please fill my mind with your peace.

DAY 3

# A Crown

*Blessed is the person who keeps on going when times are hard. After they have come through hard times, this person will receive a crown. The crown is life itself. The Lord has promised it to those who love him.*

JAMES 1:12 NIRV

Jesus, life is sometimes hard for me and for others. I don't understand why, but I trust that you are in control. I am not strong enough on my own. Please give me your strength. I can keep going because I know that you are with me. You have a good plan, and you will help me. Thank you for loving me so much.

DAY 4

# He Made Me Free

*God made us free from the power of darkness, and he brought us into the kingdom of his dear Son.*

COLOSSIANS 1:13 ICB

God, thank you for rescuing me from the power of sin and darkness. It is hard not to give in to temptation and sin. When I get mad, I need your strength to help me control my emotions and respond in the right way. Thank you for giving me the freedom to make a better choice. I am grateful that you gave me the gift of eternal life in heaven with you. That is so exciting!

I can keep going
because I know that
you are with me.

DAY 5

# Good Gifts

*Every good action and every perfect gift is from God. These good gifts come down from the Creator of the sun, moon, and stars, who does not change like their shifting shadows.*

James 1:17 NCV

God, when I look up, I see the sky full of sunshine and clouds during the day and the moon and stars at night. You are such an amazing creator. You put a colorful rainbow in the sky after it rains, and you made shooting stars that I can watch fall in the night sky. You made so many cool things for me to see and enjoy, but you love me most of all. I love you too.

DAY 6

# Life Forever

*Our hope for life forever. God promised that life to us before time began, and God does not lie.*

TITUS 1:2 ICB

God, I believe that what you said is true and you will do what you say because you don't lie. When you make a promise, you keep it. Thank you for the promise of life forever with you in heaven. I don't have to listen to the worries in my head that make me afraid about what will happen tomorrow or the next day. You hold everything in your hands.

DAY 7

# Yes and Amen

*God has made a great many promises. They are all "Yes" because of what Christ has done. So through Christ we say "Amen." We want God to receive glory.*

2 CORINTHIANS 1:20 NIRV

Jesus, you died on the cross to take away my sin so I could be close to you. That was a very special thing you did, and I want other people to know about it. Show me how to talk about you. Give me the right words to say. Help me to be brave. I want people to know that they can be forgiven from their sin just like me.

DAY 8

# Easy to See

*There are things about God that people cannot see—his eternal power and all the things that make him God. But since the beginning of the world those things have been easy to understand. They are made clear by what God has made.*

ROMANS 1:20 ICB

God, I see your creative power all around me. There are snowflakes with tiny patterns and each one is different from the next. It is so amazing to watch the lights in the sky change with a beautiful sunrise or sunset. You made giant whales eat tiny krill, and sparkling gemstones grow inside ugly rocks. It is easy to see you in all these things!

You made so many cool things, but you love me most of all.

DAY 9

# Troubles

*You will have many kinds of troubles. But when these things happen, you should be very happy. You know that these things are testing your faith. And this will give you patience.*

JAMES 1:2-3 ICB

Jesus, I know that people have tough times. Instead of being sad, I can try to be positive and learn from whatever trouble comes my way. Remind me to go to you when bad things happen. Help me to be patient while I wait for you to answer my prayers and show me what to do. I want to grow stronger and be better at dealing with trouble the next time it comes around.

DAY 10

# Heavenly Glory

*Give praise to the God who is able to keep you from falling into sin. He will bring you into his heavenly glory without any fault. He will bring you there with great joy.*

JUDE 1:24 NIRV

God, I need your power to help me make good choices and keep me from sinning. Thank you for giving your only Son, Jesus, to die on the cross and forgive my sin. There is nothing I can do that is so bad you won't forgive me. It fills my heart with joy to know that one day I will get to be with you in heaven and see you shining brightly. Until that day, please help me.

DAY 11

# Stronger and Wiser

*Even the foolishness of God is wiser than men. Even the weakness of God is stronger than men.*

1 CORINTHIANS 1:25 ICB

God, there is no one in the whole wide world who is wiser or stronger than you. You made everything, and you see everything that is going on. You have all the answers to my questions. You never make mistakes, and you are never wrong. Please make me stronger and wiser. I want to be more like you each day as I learn and grow up. I need your help.

DAY 12

# Everything We Need

*Jesus has the power of God. His power has given us everything we need to live and to serve God. We have these things because we know him. Jesus called us by his glory and goodness.*

2 PETER 1:3 ICB

Jesus, thank you that I can go to you for all my needs, and you will happily give me what I need. You are a good God who loves to give things to your children. I am so glad you are my Heavenly Father, and you chose me to be your son. Show me how I can serve you. Who can I be kind to and love more? I want to make you proud of me.

You hold everything
in your hands.

DAY 13

# Blessings in Heaven

*Now we hope for the blessings God has for his children. These blessings are kept for you in heaven. They cannot be destroyed or be spoiled or lose their beauty.*

1 PETER 1:4 ICB

God, thank you for your mercy that gives me the chance to have a new life in heaven someday. The Bible tells me that there are blessings waiting in heaven for me. Those blessings are from the sacrifice Jesus made out of love for me. I didn't earn them, and I can never lose them. They last forever. I know that I can trust your words and I look forward to those blessings someday.

DAY 14

# Full of Comfort

*God is the Father who is full of mercy and all comfort. He comforts us every time we have trouble, so when others have trouble, we can comfort them with the same comfort God gives us.*

2 CORINTHIANS 1:3-4 NCV

God, thank you for being there for me every time I have trouble. It is good to know that I am not alone and that I have you to comfort me. When I get into trouble for the mistakes and bad choices I have made, you forgive me when I say sorry. Help me to forgive and comfort other people like you forgive and comfort me.

DAY 15

# Practice Patience

*Let your patience show itself perfectly in what you do. Then you will be perfect and complete and will have everything you need.*

JAMES 1:4 NCV

Jesus, you know me better than anyone else. You see how I struggle to be patient and wait for my turn. You know how I want to rush ahead to do something fun instead of doing a good job with my chores or taking the time to practice my talents. I don't want to do a quick, sloppy job of the work I need to do just to get it done. Help me learn to be patient.

DAY 16

# Holy Spirit Power

*God loves you. And we know that he has chosen you to be his. We brought the Good News to you. But we did not use only words. We brought the Good News with power, with the Holy Spirit, and with sure knowledge that it is true.*

1 THESSALONIANS 1:4-5 ICB

Jesus, thank you for the Holy Spirit who is like a superhero with superhero power. It is so exciting to know that you can fill me up with the power to do what you want me to do. I hear stories of amazing things that happened in the Bible, and you are still doing amazing things today in the lives of your people. Teach me more about the power of the Holy Spirit.

There is no one in the whole wide world who is wiser or stronger than you.

DAY 17

# God Is Light

*Here is the message we have heard from God and now tell to you: God is light, and in him there is no darkness at all.*

1 JOHN 1:5 ICB

God, you are light! That means there is nothing bad about you. You don't try to trick me. You never lie. You are full of love. You give me good gifts. When I am sad, you help me feel joy. When I am worried, you put your peace in my mind. When I feel lonely, you are with me. Thank you for shining your light into dark places.

DAY 18

# His Children

*Because of his love, God had already decided to make us his own children through Jesus Christ. That was what he wanted and what pleased him.*

EPHESIANS 1:5 NCV

God, it is very special that you love me so much you decided to make me your child. Thank you, Jesus, for making it possible by dying on the cross to take away my sin. You do everything out of love. I want to do things that please you and show how much I love you. Please help me act like a child of God.

DAY 19

# Ask for It

*If any of you needs wisdom, you should ask God for it. He will give it to you. God gives freely to everyone and doesn't find fault.*

JAMES 1:5 NIRV

God, I am just a kid. I don't know as much as adults do. I need help making the right choice and knowing what to do. I need wisdom from you. You are full of wisdom, and you give generously to those you love. I ask you for wisdom right now to help me understand how to act more like you and how to tell other kids about you.

DAY 20

# Chosen

*"Before I formed you in your mother's body*
*I chose you.*
*Before you were born I set you apart*
*to serve me."*

JEREMIAH 1:5 NIRV

God, it is hard to imagine that you knew me before I was born. You had a plan for my life right from the very beginning, while I was still growing in my mother's tummy. Your plan for my life is special and different from your plan for other kids. You don't make mistakes. You say that I am wonderfully made. I trust your plan for me. Help me to follow you each day.

There are blessings waiting in heaven for me.

DAY 21

# Good Work

*God began doing a good work in you, and I am sure he will continue it until it is finished when Jesus Christ comes again.*

PHILIPPIANS 1:6 NCV

God, thank you for never giving up on me. Even when I can't see what you are doing, I know that you are working. Even though I don't understand what you are doing, I know you have a great plan for me. I am excited to see what you want me to do and where you want me to go when I grow up. Whatever it is, I know it will be good.

DAY 22

# Believe

*You have not seen Christ, but still you love him. You cannot see him now, but you believe in him. So you are filled with a joy that cannot be explained.*

1 PETER 1:8 NCV

Jesus, I have never seen you, but I believe you are real. I may not know what you look like, but I love you with all of my heart, and I know you love me too. I have learned about how good you are, and I see some of the ways you love me by giving me what I need and making me feel better. Continue to show me your love and help me understand you more.

DAY 23

# Live in the Light

*God is in the light. We should live in the light, too. If we live in the light, we share fellowship with each other. And when we live in the light, the blood of the death of Jesus, God's Son, is making us clean from every sin.*

1 JOHN 1:7 ICB

God, here is another verse that says you are the light, and that I should live in the light. Help me to choose what you would choose to do or not do. I want to be like you. Show me how to be kind and caring to people. Teach me to be patient and control myself. Thank you, Jesus, for dying on the cross so that you could wash away my sin and make my heart clean.

DAY 24

# Real Faith

*Your troubles have come in order to prove that your faith is real. Your faith is worth more than gold. That's because gold can pass away even when fire has made it pure. Your faith is meant to bring praise, honor and glory to God.*

1 PETER 1:7 NIRV

Jesus, I have faith in you by believing that you are real even though I can't see you. I believe that you are the Son of God who died and had the power to come back to life to save me. I know that there is trouble in the world. I also know that you will make my faith grow stronger every time you help me go through hard times in my life. You deserve all of my praise.

You know me better
than anyone else.

DAY 25

# A Powerful Gift

*God did not give us a spirit that makes us afraid. He gave us a spirit of power and love and self-control.*

2 Timothy 1:7 ICB

God, thank you for giving me your Holy Spirit. What a powerful gift! I don't have to be afraid. The Holy Spirit lives in my heart and is with me wherever I go. That brings me peace, joy, comfort, strength, hope, and love. It helps me control my feelings and emotions and gives me wisdom to make better choices. Thank you!

DAY 26

# Set Free

*We have been set free because of what Christ has done. Because he bled and died our sins have been forgiven.*

EPHESIANS 1:7 NIRV

Jesus, thank you so much for dying on the cross so that I could be free from the darkness of sin. It was a very painful way to die. I am sorry that you had to suffer for me, and I am very grateful that you did that. I am starting to see how much you love me. Please forgive me for anything wrong I have done today. Thank you for your forgiveness.

DAY 27

# Always Good

*The LORD is good.*
*When people are in trouble,*
*they can go to him for safety.*
*He takes good care of those*
*who trust in him.*

NAHUM 1:7 NIRV

God, you are so good to me. You help me when I am in trouble. You protect my mind from worry and fear. You provide me with a home and food and family who watch over me. You give me friends who make me laugh. No matter what happens, I know that you will take care of me because you always have. You are good.

DAY 28

# Spirit Power

*"When the Holy Spirit comes to you, you will receive power."*

ACTS 1:8 NCV

Jesus, you said these words to the first believers, and your words are still for me today. Open my ears to hear you speaking to me. Open my eyes to see you working. I want to know you more. I want to feel your love every day of my life. Fill me up with your power that will help me do great things for you that I could never do on my own.

You are still doing amazing things today.

DAY 29

# Don't Be Afraid

*"Don't be afraid of anyone, because I am with you. I will protect you," says the Lord.*

JEREMIAH 1:8 ICB

God, you are like a giant shield protecting me from the enemy. You are the only one who can truly protect me all of the time. Help me to be brave when the enemy attacks my mind with fear and lies. Show me what is true and what is not. Thank you for never leaving me alone, for making me brave when I am afraid, and for comforting me when I get hurt.

DAY 30

# Mighty One

*"I am the Alpha and the Omega, the Beginning and the End," says the Lord God. "I am the God who is, and who was, and who will come. I am the Mighty One."*

REVELATION 1:8 NIRV

God, you have always been here, from the beginning to the end. It is hard to imagine your greatness. I try to think of all the awesome things you have done for me and my family and friends. Thank you for using your power to bless and protect me. I will only worship you. There is no one else as mighty as you. There is nothing you cannot do.

DAY 31

# Clean

*If we confess our sins, he will forgive our sins. We can trust God. He does what is right. He will make us clean from all the wrongs we have done.*

1 JOHN 1:9 ICB

God, thank you for always being willing to listen to me. I confess my sin and say sorry for the bad choices I make. I am so grateful that you forgive me, no matter what I do. You are loving, not mean and grumpy. Once you forgive me, I am made clean from the wrong things I have done. Thank you for setting me free from sin.

DAY 32

# Be Strong and Brave

*"Here is what I am commanding you to do. Be strong and brave. Do not be afraid. Do not lose hope. I am the LORD your God. I will be with you everywhere you go."*

JOSHUA 1:9 NIRV

Jesus, I hear you say in this verse to be strong and brave, not to be afraid, not to lose hope, and that you are with me wherever I go. That makes me feel safe and secure. This verse comes from the book of Joshua, who led the Israelites in many battles, including the battle of Jericho where you made the city walls come tumbling down. I will try to be brave like Joshua.

When I feel lonely,
you are with me.

DAY 33

# Good Care

*"You gave me life. You were kind to me. You took good care of me. You watched over me."*

JOB 10:12 NIRV

God, thank you for giving me life. You made me a boy and created me just the way you wanted me to look. You call me your beloved child because of how special I am to you. I love that! Thank you for giving me a family who takes care of me and watches over me. Thank you for giving me friends who are kind to me. You have filled my life with your love.

DAY 34

# A Way Out

*You are tempted in the same way all other human beings are. God is faithful. He will not let you be tempted any more than you can take. But when you are tempted, God will give you a way out. Then you will be able to deal with it.*

1 CORINTHIANS 10:13 NIRV

God, there are times when I am tempted to lose control of my emotions and say things out of anger. Thank you for never leaving me to fight those battles on my own. When I pray and ask you for help, you will give me a way out. Help me know how to deal with anger the right way.

DAY 35

# Made Holy

*With one sacrifice he made perfect forever those who are being made holy.*

HEBREWS 10:14 NCV

Jesus, you are holy and perfect. You never did one bad thing. I don't have to be perfect though. I can never be perfect. Because of the sacrifice you made by dying on the cross, you took away my sin and made me holy. That is a big deal. Thank you for doing that. I will try to please you by being good and showing love to those around me.

DAY 36

# He Sees

*Lord, surely you see these cruel and evil things.*
*Look at them and do something.*
*People in trouble look to you for help.*
*You are the one who helps the orphans.*

PSALM 10:14 ICB

God, there are sad things happening in the world right now. People are sick and dying. There are children without parents. People are in trouble, and they need help. I'm just a kid. What can I do? I can pray. I pray that you will heal and comfort those who need it. You see everything. You love everyone. Please help them.

You do everything
out of love.

DAY 37

# Hold On

*Let us hold firmly to the hope that we have confessed, because we can trust God to do what he promised.*

HEBREWS 10:23 NCV

God, when I asked you into my heart, you put hope inside of me. Instead of feeling worried or afraid when trouble comes along, I will stand firm like a strong oak tree. I will not let fear or worry take away my hope. I feel your peace. I will not forget the ways you have been there for me. I will not let go of hope. You will do what you have promised to do.

DAY 38

# Happiness

*A good person can look forward to happiness,*
*but an evil person can expect nothing.*

PROVERBS 10:28 NCV

God, this verse says that the reward for being good is happiness. I like to feel happy. Evil people who purposely do bad things get nothing. *Nothing!* That sounds terrible. For people who love and serve you, there is a reward that is better than anyone can imagine. That is what I want. Help me to be a good person who does good things for you and enjoys the reward of happiness.

DAY 39

# Little Things Matter

*"God even knows how many hairs are on your head. So don't be afraid. You are worth much more than many sparrows."*

MATTHEW 10:30-31 NCV

Jesus, thank you for caring about the details in my life. You know the exact number of hairs on my head. My mom and dad don't even know that. You take care of the birds in the air, the fish in the sea, and every living thing. That includes me! I can trust that you will take care of the little things in my life as well as the big stuff.

DAY 40

# You Belong to Me

*"All those who stand before others and say they believe in me, I will say before my Father in heaven that they belong to me."*

MATTHEW 10:32 NCV

Jesus, I believe in you, and I will not be afraid to tell other people that I believe in you. It is good to know that you tell your Father in heaven that I belong to you. I give you my heart, and you fill it with your peace. That takes away my fears and calms my worries. There is no one better to me than you. I am so glad that I belong to you.

You had a plan for
my life right from
the very beginning.

DAY 41

# The Same

*"I really understand now that to God every person is the same. God accepts anyone who worships him and does what is right. It is not important what country a person comes from."*

ACTS 10:34–35 ICB

God, I am glad that you don't have favorites. You love each person with enough love to go around for everyone. Every person in the world is loved by you. You accept those who worship you into the family of God. There is a chance for anyone to confess their sins and accept you as their Savior. Every person is someone you love.

DAY 42

# Don't Lose Courage

*Do not lose the courage that you had in the past. It has a great reward.*

HEBREWS 10:35 ICB

Jesus, I don't want to lose the courage I have from you. When I am afraid, and it is hard to understand what is going on, remind me that you are beside me. You give me your power to be strong, even if I don't feel strong. You have helped me before and you will keep helping me. I don't have to be afraid because you win in the end.

DAY 43

# Be Faithful

*You need to be faithful. Then you will do what God wants. You will receive what he has promised.*

HEBREWS 10:36 NIRV

God, the Bible is full of your promises. I made a promise to follow you when I asked you into my heart as my Lord and Savior. I want to be faithful and not give up when it's hard or when I'm tired of doing what's right. I trust you to lead me to do what you want me to do. When I make a mistake, I will come back to you and try again.

DAY 44

# On and On

*The LORD is good. His love is forever,*
*and his loyalty goes on and on.*

PSALM 100:5 NCV

God, it is a wonderful thing that your love never ends. It goes on and on for all eternity. I have a hard time understanding how long eternity is, but that doesn't matter. I know that you love me a whole bunch, and you will never stop loving me. You are loyal. You will never give up or walk away from me. You keep giving me good things, and I am thankful for each one.

There is nothing
you cannot do.

DAY 45

# He Answers

*He will answer the prayers of the needy.*
*He will not reject their prayers.*

PSALM 102:17 ICB

God, thank you for hearing every one of my prayers and for answering them. Even if I have to wait a while for you to answer, I know that you will. I won't stop praying. I won't stop asking. Only you have the power to change the things that need to change and fix the things that need fixing. No prayer is too big for you or too silly. Thanks for caring.

DAY 46

# Look Up

*As high as the sky is above the earth,*
*so great is his love for those who respect him.*

PSALM 103:11 NCV

Jesus, when I look up into the sky, I sometimes see airplanes flying way up high. You say in this verse that your love for me is as high as the sky. That's incredible! When I look at the sky, I will think of how great your love is. I will respect you by being careful with my words, making good choices, and obeying you.

DAY 47

# A Father's Love

*A father is tender and kind to his children. In the same way, the LORD is tender and kind to those who have respect for him.*

PSALM 103:13 NIRV

God, I am grateful that you are kind and gentle to your children. You are a good father who cares for his family. Thank you for accepting me into your family and calling me your child. Show me how to be respectful toward you. I want to listen and obey you and not be naughty. I want you to be proud of me and how I behave.

DAY 48

# Wonderful God

*I will praise the* LORD.
*I won't forget anything he does for me.*
*He forgives all my sins.*
*He heals all my sicknesses.*

PSALM 103:2-3 NIRV

God, I will not forget the wonderful things you have done for me. I think about them now. You created me and gave me life. You forgive all my sins and make me holy, so that I can spend eternity with you in heaven. You give me your Holy Spirit to comfort me and make me strong. You will never stop loving me. You always listen to me. I praise you for so many things!

You have filled my life
with your love.

DAY 49

# Crowned with Life

*His faithful and tender love makes*
*me feel like a king.*
*He satisfies me with the good things I desire.*

PSALM 103:4-5 NIRV

Jesus, thank you for giving me good things. You don't just give me what I need, you also give me what I like. I feel like a special king who receives lots of good gifts. Because you made me a part of the family of God, I get to be a son of the King of Heaven. You even have a crown for me. That is exciting news. Thank you!

DAY 50

# Slow to Anger

*The LORD shows mercy and is kind.*
*He does not become angry quickly,*
*and he has great love.*

PSALM 103:8 ICB

God, there is no one else as patient and kind as you. You don't blow up at people when you get mad. You have control of your emotions. It is good to know that I don't have to be afraid of you even when I mess up and do something wrong. Thank you for your mercy and great love that lets me start over again.

DAY 51

# Chain Breaker

*He brought them out of their gloom*
*and darkness*
*and broke their chains.*

Psalm 107:14 NCV

Jesus, you are my hero. You fight for my freedom. Sin can make me feel like a prisoner with chains on, and I'm not able to break free from making bad choices. But you can set me free and give me your strength to say no to bad things. I will listen to you as you show me what to do. Thank you for rescuing me.

DAY 52

# Food and Water

*He gives those who are thirsty*
*all the water they want.*
*He gives those who are hungry*
*all the good food they can eat.*

PSALM 107:9 NIRV

Jesus, you don't just give a little bit. You give until I am satisfied. When I ask you for something, you are happy. Sometimes your answer is yes, and sometimes you say no because you have something better for me. Other times you say not yet. While I wait for you to answer my prayers, I will trust you to do what's best for me.

You see everything.
You love everyone.

DAY 53

# A Right Heart

*God, my heart is right.*
*I will sing and praise you with all my being.*

PSALM 108:1 ICB

God, I want my heart to be pleasing to you. Fill my heart with your love, so I can be kind to others. Help me be thankful for all the good things you put in my life. Each day has lots of reasons to praise you: sunshine to play outside or rain to make gardens grow. I will sing to you because you deserve to be praised for what you do.

DAY 54

# Faith

*Faith means being sure of the things we hope for and knowing that something is real even if we do not see it.*

HEBREWS 11:1 NCV

Jesus, you are real to me even if someone else doesn't believe in you. Even if my faith is strong and sure, I can still have questions about things I don't understand. Thank you that you don't change. You keep your promises, so I can still hope for things to get better. I believe that you are a part of my life each day and you have a good plan for me.

DAY 55

# Ask and Believe

*"I tell you to believe that you have received the things you ask for in prayer, and God will give them to you."*

MARK 11:24 NCV

Jesus, I bring you my questions, my wants, my needs, my hopes, and my dreams. Thank you for not thinking they are silly things to ask for. Thank you for seeing my heart and knowing what I am thinking and feeling. I choose to believe that you will answer my prayers because you are good to me. I know you can do anything.

DAY 56

# Live Forever

*"I am the resurrection and the life. Anyone who believes in me will live, even if they die. And whoever lives by believing in me will never die."*

JOHN 11:25-26 NIRV

Jesus, you have amazing power that brought you back to life after you died on the cross. I am so thankful that because I believe in you, I get to live forever in heaven with you once my life on earth is over. I don't need to be afraid of dying. This is what you mean when you say anyone who believes in you will live and never die. Thank you.

You will do what you have promised to do.

DAY 57

# Heavy Load

*"Come to me, all of you who are tired and have heavy loads. I will give you rest."*

MATTHEW 11:28 ICB

Jesus, thank you for giving me rest when I need it. I get tired from being busy with school, church, and other activities. My brain gets tired from all the learning, and my heart gets tired sometimes from being mad or sad or worried. It feels like I am carrying a heavy load. When I pray to you, I can give you my heavy load and trade it for your peace.

DAY 58

# Be a Servant

*"Become my servants and learn from me. I am gentle and free of pride. You will find rest for your souls."*

MATTHEW 11:29 NCV

Jesus, you are smarter than everyone, but you are humble and gentle, not rude or bossy. You are powerful. There is nothing you can't do. You chose to leave heaven and be a servant to everyone on earth. You healed the sick, had dinner with people who no one else liked, and you talked to people who made bad choices. I want to learn from you and serve others like you did.

DAY 59

# What We See

*It is by faith we understand that the whole world was made by God's command. This means that what we see was made by something that cannot be seen.*

HEBREWS 11:3 ICB

God, even though I did not see you create the universe, I believe that the whole world was made by you. I also believe that you created me for a special purpose. My faith grows stronger when I look at everything you made and think of how you created it just by your words. I believe that you continue to do amazing things even today that I cannot see.

DAY 60

# Come to Him

*Without faith no one can please God. Anyone who comes to God must believe that he is real and that he rewards those who truly want to find him.*

HEBREWS 11:6 NCV

God, thank you that I can come to you with questions and a heart full of faith. Just because I am curious, it doesn't mean I don't have faith. I am trying to understand and learn about you. You are a good teacher who likes it when I talk to you about what's on my mind. Thank you for letting me be free to share my thoughts and worries with you.

There is no one better to me than you.

DAY 61

# Don't Lose Faith

*"The person who does not lose faith because of me is blessed."*

MATTHEW 11:6 ICB

Jesus, you did many amazing miracles while you were here on earth. That would've been so cool to see! It's sad to know there were people who got mad at what you were doing. Maybe they were jealous. Help me to be strong and confident to defend my faith when others make fun of it. I don't want to be shy or embarrassed that I believe in you.

DAY 62

# Right and True

*He is faithful and right in everything he does. All his rules can be trusted.*

PSALM 111:7 NIRV

God, I know that you are fair, honest, and good because you are perfect. I can trust you to always keep your promises and tell the truth. Help me to do the same. I am not perfect, but I will try my best to be as good as I can be. You give me the power of the Holy Spirit to help me. Your rules are there to protect me. Thank you for your goodness.

DAY 63

# Shine a Light

*A light shines in the dark for honest people, for those who are merciful and kind and good.*

PSALM 112:4 NCV

Jesus, when I spend time with you, I learn how to be a good person and become more like you. You won't run out of mercy for me when I make the same mistakes. You are good to me even when I'm not good to you. Shine the light of your love in my heart and help me to be merciful, kind, and good to others like you are to me.

DAY 64

# Relax

*I said to myself, "Relax,*
*because the Lord takes care of you."*

PSALM 116:7 ICB

God, when the enemy tries to take away my peace and fill my mind with worries, I will remember the words in this verse. I will tell myself to relax and remind myself of the ways you have already taken care of me. Because you have done it before, I know you will take care of me right now too. Help me relax as I sit here and talk to you.

Every person is
someone you love.

DAY 65

# Everlasting

*The Lord loves us very much.*
*His truth is everlasting.*
*Praise the Lord!*

PSALM 117:2 ICB

God, I praise you because of how much you love me. It is hard to understand how great your love is. Your love changes me, and my love grows for you. Your love lasts forever. It doesn't change based on what kind of mood you are in. You don't change from the wonderful, perfect God you already are. I thank you for your everlasting love.

DAY 66

# Trust God

*It is better to go to the LORD for safety than to trust in mere human beings.*

PSALM 118:8 NIRV

God, when I am afraid, I usually run to my mom or dad, but help me to remember I can run to you too. I can tell you what I am afraid of. I can sit quietly on my bed and listen for you to tell me what I need to hear. I am safe with you. I can trust you. You are with me. You help me feel better.

DAY 67

# Shield of Safety

*You are my place of safety.*
*You are like a shield that keeps me safe.*
*I have put my hope in your word..*

PSALM 119:114 NIRV

God, you are a shield around me keeping me safe. You defend me when lies are spoken about me. You protect me from things I cannot see. Instead of getting stuck in fear, I can stand tall behind your shield of safety. Help me to remember your words in the Bible that are true. You will defeat the lies of the enemy. Your words fill my heart and mind with hope.

DAY 68

# Near to Me

*LORD, you are near.*
*All your commands are true.*

PSALM 119:151 NIRV

God, I love that you are near to me. You are close by anytime I need you. I can't see you, but I can feel your love. You help me calm down. Your joy can change my mood from crabby to happy when I talk to you and give you my attention. Thank you for speaking to me through your Word. I want to feel close to you.

I don't have to be afraid because you win in the end.

DAY 69

# Fairness

*Your words are true from the start,*
*and all your laws will be fair forever.*

Psalm 119:160 NCV

God, you see the evil in the world and what evil people are doing. It makes me feel safe to know you see what's going on, and I can trust you to take care of it. You are fair. You will punish the people doing bad things. I am so grateful that you are more powerful than the bad people in this world. You are full of truth and fairness. You are the best judge.

DAY 70

# True Peace

*Those who love your teachings*
*will find true peace.*
*Nothing will defeat them.*

PSALM 119:165 ICB

Jesus, help me to learn and remember your teachings in the Bible. Your words will quiet the worries in my mind and replace them with peaceful thoughts. You give me the freedom to choose who to listen to: you or the enemy, truth or lies. Even if I make mistakes, you forgive me. I am getting better at knowing the truth as I learn more from you.

DAY 71

# You Promised

*Even when I suffer, I am comforted because you promised to keep me alive.*

PSALM 119:50 NIRV

God, I am comforted to know you are faithful and will never disappoint me. You are reliable. I can count on you to keep your promises. You promised never to destroy the earth again in a flood, and you put a rainbow in the sky as a reminder. Thank you that I get to see your promise like that. Even when I get sick, I won't be afraid. You are with me.

DAY 72

# What You Do

*Many good things come from what people say. And the work of their hands rewards them.*

PROVERBS 12:14 NIRV

God, help me to be wise in what I say and do. I don't want to do sloppy work. I want you to be proud of me for doing a good job. When I am tempted to rush through my work, remind me to slow down and do my best. When I want to speak before I think, remind me to be wise and choose my words carefully. I don't want to miss out on a reward from you.

You will never give up
or walk away from me.

DAY 73

# Each Part

*If the whole body were an eye, how could it hear? If the whole body were an ear, how could it smell? God has placed each part in the body just as he wanted it to be.*

1 CORINTHIANS 12:17-18 NIRV

God, it is so interesting how you created people. You made me special, just the way you wanted me to be. Thank you for the abilities you gave me. You have a specific purpose for my life. It's no good to wish I was like someone else. What a waste of time. Help me to become who you want me to be.

DAY 74

# Faith Journey

*Let us keep looking to Jesus. He is the one who started this journey of faith. And he is the one who completes the journey of faith.*

HEBREWS 12:2 NIRV

Jesus, you are the best example of how to live my life. Life is a journey, and people with faith have you as their guide. You showed me how to forgive people who say mean things. You made a way for me to have eternal life in heaven by dying on the cross and forgiving my sins. I want to follow you. Guide me on my faith journey through life.

DAY 75

# He Saves Me

*"God is the one who saves me;*
*I will trust him and not be afraid.*
*The* L*ORD, the* L*ORD gives me strength and*
*makes me sing."*

ISAIAH 12:2 NCV

God, thank you for saving me. The enemy tries really hard to tempt me to sin and make bad choices. Please give me strength to not fall for the enemy's tricks. I know I can trust you to help me. I don't have to be afraid anymore. I will sing songs about how good and wonderful you are. You are my Savior. I trust you to take care of me.

DAY 76

# Never Abandoned

*The LORD won't leave his people. Instead, he was pleased to make you his own people.*

1 SAMUEL 12:22 ICB

God, it is so good to know that you will never leave me. I see stories about dogs that are left by their owners. The dogs look sick, dirty, sad, and hungry. You will never abandon me. You stay by my side and lead me where I should go. You give me everything I need. You never stop loving me. Thank you!

I trust you to do
what's best for me.

DAY 77

# With Respect

*We are receiving a kingdom that can't be shaken. So let us be thankful. Then we can worship God in a way that pleases him. Let us worship him with deep respect and wonder.*

HEBREWS 12:28 NIRV

God, show me how to worship you with respect and wonder. I am amazed at all you created. I could make a long list of the good things you have given me, and I am so thankful. One day I will join you in heaven with all the other people who followed you, and we will worship you together. You deserve it. You are powerful, wise, fair, honest, and good. There is no one like you.

DAY 78

# Lying Lips

*The Lord will stop those lying lips.*
*He will cut off those bragging tongues.*

PSALM 12:3 ICB

God, remind me to go to you when I fall into the trap of lying. It is a terrible feeling when I get caught in a lie. I don't want to be a liar. Thank you for forgiving me when I mess up. I don't want to brag either. I don't want to be someone who only likes to talk about myself. Help me to speak words that are true and kind.

DAY 79

# Don't Worry

*"Don't always think about what you will eat or what you will drink, and don't keep worrying. All the people in the world are trying to get these things, and your Father knows you need them."*

LUKE 12:29-30 NCV

Jesus, people all around the world tend to worry. I do too sometimes. Instead of wasting time worrying about things that may or may not happen, I will turn my worries into prayers. When a worry pops into my head, I will pray and give that worry to you. All of my problems are safe in your hands. You can solve any problem, and you know what's best for me. I love you.

DAY 80

# Differences

*There are different ways that God works through people but the same God. God works in all of us in everything we do.*

1 CORINTHIANS 12:6 NCV

God, I'm grateful that you don't do the same thing over and over. That would be boring, like a factory machine making the same toy one after another. You made each person different, and there are different ways you work in each person. Teachers, doctors, farmers, and artists are all different. It is interesting to see how creative you are. You are an amazing inventor of people!

DAY 81

# Power in Weakness

*"My grace is enough for you. When you are weak, my power is made perfect in you."*

2 CORINTHIANS 12:9 NCV

God, as I grow older, I can do more things on my own, but there are still areas where I am weak. Those are the areas that I need your strength to help me. Weakness isn't always a bad thing. It can be a chance for me to see your power at work. If I could do everything, then I would miss seeing your power, and others would miss it too. That would be sad.

DAY 82

# Love and Peace

*Be joyful! Work to make things right with one another. Help one another and agree with one another. Live in peace. And the God who gives love and peace will be with you.*

2 Corinthians 13:11 NIRV

Jesus, you are also called the Prince of Peace. You make peace and you want me to do that too. Nobody likes to be around people who argue a lot. Help me not to make people angry. Show me what to say and when to say it. I need to get filled up with your love each morning, so I have enough love to give to others.

I give you my heavy load and trade it for your peace.

DAY 83

# Things that Last

*The three most important things to have are faith, hope and love. But the greatest of them is love.*

1 CORINTHIANS 13:13 NIRV

Jesus, I need all three of these things: faith, hope, and love. Help me grow stronger in my faith, so I can talk to people about you and do the big things you have created me to do. Make me wise, so I won't believe lies and doubt the good future you promise me. Show you how much you love me and everyone else in the world.

DAY 84

# Be Like You

*Whoever spends time with wise people*
*will become wise.*
*But whoever makes friends with fools*
*will suffer.*

Proverbs 13:20 ICB

God, I will be like the people I am around. If I spend a lot of time with friends who make good choices, then I will become like them. If I spend a lot of time with friends who make bad choices, then I will suffer the consequences of bad behavior. Please help me carefully choose friends who are wise.

DAY 85

# Rewarded

*Trouble always comes to sinners,*
*but good people enjoy success.*

PROVERBS 13:21 NCV

God, it says it right here in this verse that I will get in trouble when I purposely sin. But it also says that I will enjoy success for being good. I get rewarded for good behavior. That makes sense. When I am deciding whether to make a good choice or a bad one, please help me. I want the reward that comes to good people.

DAY 86

# Loving Money

*Keep your lives free from the love of money. And be satisfied with what you have. God has said, "I will never leave you; I will never abandon you."*

HEBREWS 13:5 ICB

God, I trust you will keep providing for me and my family because you always have. Even though we need money to buy things, please help me be grateful for what you have already given me. Help me to be satisfied with what I have and keep me from loving money more than I love you.

DAY 87

# Forever the Same

*Jesus Christ is the same yesterday, today, and forever.*

HEBREWS 13:8 ICB

Jesus, the Bible is full of stories where you gave your attention, care, and healing power. You are full of that same love and kindness today. You do not turn away from helping poor people or ignore those in need. Your forgiveness is for anyone who apologizes for their sin. That is good news for me. Thank you.

DAY 88

# Don't Stop

*LORD, you will show that I was right*
*to trust you.*
*LORD, your faithful love continues forever.*
*You have done so much for us,*
*so don't stop now.*

PSALM 138:8 NIRV

God, thank you for your faithful love that never runs out. I trust you and your plans for my life. Help me not to worry but trust you to handle each problem. I hand off my worries to you. You can do what I can't do. You are powerful enough to fix things even when I make mistakes. You will never change. Thank you for always helping me.

Your love lasts forever.

DAY 89

# Even Greater

*"Anyone who believes in me will do the works I have been doing. In fact, they will do even greater things. That's because I am going to the Father."*

JOHN 14:12 NIRV

Jesus, you have shown me how to be like you. You tell me to have compassion for others and show mercy by forgiving those who hurt me. You have also shown me that God has work for me to do here. Help me to share your love with everyone. I need the Holy Spirit's power to do even greater things.

DAY 90

# In Jesus' Name

*"If you ask for anything in my name, I will do it for you. Then the Father's glory will be shown through the Son."*

JOHN 14:13 ICB

Jesus, I have asked for things from you, and when they match what you want for me, then I know you will do it. I pray in your name. I know there is power in your name, and I want to give you the glory for the things I am praying about. I know you are happy to do things for me, and it is even better when God receives the glory.

DAY 91

# Stay Still

*"The LORD will fight for you. Just be still."*

EXODUS 14:14 NIRV

God, I trust you to fight for me, so I don't have to worry or try to defend myself when someone says untrue things about me. Instead of getting mad and rushing into an argument, I will calm myself and rely on you to show me what to do and what to say. You know my heart and what bothers me. Help me to let go of bad feelings and let you change my heart.

DAY 92

# Orphans

*"I will not leave you all alone like orphans; I will come back to you."*

JOHN 14:18 NCV

Jesus, I am never alone because you are always with me. You are the best person I know. You love me so much that you will never walk away from me even when I misbehave. Some kids don't have a mom or dad, but you are always with them. You don't forget about them. You promise to come back to earth someday for everyone who loves you.

DAY 93

# Many Rooms

*"There are many rooms in my Father's house;
I would not tell you this if it were not true.
I am going there to prepare a place for you."*

JOHN 14:2 ICB

Jesus, it is exciting to hear you talk about our home in heaven. It has many rooms for everyone. Sometimes I wonder what my room will look like. Help me to love those who don't know you. I want to tell them about you, so your family will grow bigger and bigger. There is no limit to your love or to our home in heaven.

DAY 94

# The Helper

*"The Helper will teach you everything and will cause you to remember all that I told you. This Helper is the Holy Spirit whom the Father will send in my name."*

JOHN 14:26 NCV

Jesus, thank you for giving me a helper in the Holy Spirit. He is like a teacher who reminds me of what I have learned. He is in my heart to lead me and guide me. Thank you for your comfort when I am sad, for strength to say no to sin, and for wisdom to pick good friends. I need your help every day.

I can stand tall behind your shield of safety.

DAY 95

# Respect the Lord

*Those who respect the LORD will have security, and their children will be protected.*

PROVERBS 14:26 NCV

Heavenly Father, you make me feel safe and secure. You are all powerful. You will never stop loving me or protecting me. You don't change. You will do what you say you will do. Show me how to respect you. I want to do what pleases you. I want to make you proud. I am so glad that I am yours.

DAY 96

# My Peace

*"I leave my peace with you. I give my peace to you. I do not give it to you as the world does. Do not let your hearts be troubled. And do not be afraid."*

JOHN 14:27 NIRV

Jesus, I am so grateful that you give freely without demanding anything in return. You don't take back what you have given. You offer your peace when my heart is troubled because you are full of compassion. I can rest quietly when I sit with you and pray. Help me to not be afraid. I want to be brave for you.

DAY 97

# Fountain of Water

*Respect for the Lord gives life.*
*It is like a fountain of water that can save people from death.*

PROVERBS 14:27 ICB

God, you created my body to need water every day. Water can save people from death. It gives life. You also give life—eternal life. That's pretty amazing. I want you to know that I respect you a lot. Help me to show self-control, choosing my words carefully and doing what I am told. You are my God and my leader.

DAY 98

# Coming Back

*"After I go and prepare a place for you, I will come back and take you to be with me so that you may be where I am."*

JOHN 14:3 NCV

Jesus, thank you for promising to return one day and take me to be with you. That will be such a special day for those who love and follow you. Help me grow into who you want me to be. Let people see you shining through me. Thank you for giving me what I need. Forgive me for the times I have ignored you. I am excited for you to come back.

DAY 99

# God of Peace

*God is not a God of confusion but a God of peace.*

1 CORINTHIANS 14:33 NCV

Jesus, please fill my mind with your wisdom. I might not understand everything in the Bible, but you have given me grownups who can help teach me, answer my questions, and pray for me. When I am anxious and afraid, please calm me down with your peaceful presence. Help me to take a few deep breaths and focus on you.

DAY 100

# The Way

*"I am the way, the truth, and the life. No one comes to the Father except through me."*

JOHN 14:6 NIRV

Jesus, it is a relief to know that I can come straight to you. I don't have to wait in line or come back when you're not busy. I can be open with you about anything. There is nothing I need to hide because you are full of. You show me how to get to heaven. You tell me the truth, and you give me eternal life. I love you, Jesus.